Have It ALL

RECIPES FOR PERPETUAL SUCCESS

Nev Kraguljevic

ISBN: 978-1792896385

Dedicated to:

My Mom
whose actions and love changed my life

Courtney Bowers, N.D.
whose kindness transformed my habits

My Nephew Matija & Niece Kalina
who have taught me how to selflessly love

Table of Contents

To get the most out of this book, make sure you interact with it:

- Highlight or underline pieces that speak to you
- Answer the questions
- Take notes (plenty of blank pages left for that purpose)
- Use your smart phone to scan the QR Codes to watch videos

Most smart phone cameras already have a capability to read the QR code. Simply point your camera at the code and the phone will do the rest.

If you discover that your phone's camera does not allow for that, look at your app store for a QR code reader and download one (they are typically free). Then follow the app instructions on how to use it.

Introduction

For over twenty years I have been living my purpose and that is to be of service to others and to serve the humanity, to help make this world a bit better place.

I believe that everyone's purpose in life is to serve humanity, however different our ways may be. We all have different talents that make us uniquely beautiful and it is our job to learn what those talents are and how to best use them so that when we leave this life, the world is better because we were here, however long that may be.

I have transformed myself and my life in many different ways, and in some ways one could even say I have been reborn, but not in the religious sort of way. Rather as a shift that my body and mind have taken over the course of my lifetime.

Today, the buzz word for the transformation is "pivot" and one could say I have "pivoted" quite a few times.

I have gone from being a member of traditionally disadvantaged group to being a member of the traditionally advantaged group, from living in a place of poverty to a place of abundance, where any dream can come true, as long as you have it.

This not only changed how others viewed and interacted with me, but it also changed how I viewed myself. The world around me and how I interact with it has shifted; with it, I have continued to grow and evolve.

Like me, all people, other living things, and the world in general, are continuously changing and evolving. The way we see ourselves and the way we show up in the world changes all the time. This change happens with or without our active participation. Knowing that there is this constant change, you can choose to actively participate and thus ensure that the change happening is the one of growth as oppose to the one of decay. Yes, you are that powerful!

I have been so blessed to have had an amazing journey up to this point of my life and I believe the fun is just about to begin. I haven't always felt that way and it took some serious internal work to be where I am today, in addition to receiving the support from the outside. From it all, I have learned a lot and I continue to learn every day. For all that has happened, I am grateful for and there is not a single thing I would change as it all has made me who I am today.

I know that there will be challenges coming up in the future, but because of my personal growth, I am now certain all of them are for the better and I welcome it all. Why? Because that is the story I chose to tell myself.

I have spent a lot of time and money educating myself and I will most likely continue to do so for as long as I live. I have attended and continue to attend many seminars, workshops, conferences, and I have read and continue to read many books on and I am privileged to have a long list of mentors, some alive and some dead, whom I use daily to inspire and guide me. I have been teaching and training others on leadership, success, diversity, and personal finance, for over 15 years and in that time I have worked with tens of thousands of individuals.

One day, after mediation, a thought came to me that I must share what I have learned and what I know in a way that can help more people, outside my, often limited seating events. The challenge was to make it simple to grasp, easy to apply, personal, and portable. I took on that challenge and this is what came out (pun intended).

I believe that everyone has a genius inside them, so I have provided areas for you to add things that work for you. This way, this booklet truly can become your personal success recipe. Make it your own and read it daily. Create time in your day to consider what you have read and how you can apply it in your life. I hope it serves you well and get ready for amazing things to happen in your life.

Nev K.

People Are Not Bread

You might have looked at the cover of this book and thought to yourself "what does a story have to do with success and did this Nev K-whatever person really dare state there's a recipe for it all?"

In this book, I will share with you some of the most profound and most significant ingredients you will need in order to become successful.

If you've ever baked or cooked anything, you know that there is a recipe that explains what ingredients you need, how to mix them, how to prepare, cook, cool, serve, etc. Perhaps you had a Betty Crocker book that you followed (for the younger generation, perhaps you "Googled" the recipe on your phone, tablet, or watch). In either case, those recipes are very particular (borderline limiting) for those of us that like to play and be adventurous in our kitchens.

If you have grown up with a mother or perhaps a grandmother like mine, then your recipes will look quite a bit different. Here in the United States I would see a cup of flour and 2 TBSP butter. Back home, my mom would grab a utensil, whichever happen to be close by and clean, and scoop up some flour. Then she'd take a knife and lop off some butter.

I remember when she was alive, I would sometimes call her to ask for a recipe how to make my favorite childhood meal or treat. As we talk she would get into her story say "ugh, that much" and snap her fingers completely forgetting I'm on the phone and cannot see her making the motion to indicate perhaps a pinch.

Her cooking style and her recipes are old school, where a pinch was a measure people knew how to incorporate into their cooking. It left room for individualization, for weather, pressure, altitude, differential in oven temperatures, and of course, creativity!

You may think that the recipe I'm providing is here is similar to Betty Crocker book, where ingredients are specific, temperature never varies, and the amounts are so precisely measured, ability to get creative simply does not exist. For making of the bread or cake, those can be very helpful.

But people are not bread!

Even though we have many similarities, we are also very different, and we respond in different ways to stimuli and learning. So, this book of success recipes is meant for you to play around with and discover what actually works for you and in what manner.

What I mean by that is that you might want to consider reading the whole thing first, fully open-minded (good thing it's a small book, huh?) and become familiar with the ingredients contained within it: affirmations, beliefs, story, excuses, pain, change, acceptance and self-love, growth, fear, warrior, your life's mission, success, and cultural background. Once you understand the underlying ingredients for success, you'll be able to determine which of them you need more or less of, in what order and in what combination. Some things will trigger you right away all on their own, and others you will need to combine to get the full effect.

Continuing with the food analogy, since that is how we started, my version of the success recipes is really more of the cafeteria style rather than the five-course served meal.

Why?

You know yourself better than anyone else does. You know how much you can eat, even if at times you chew off more than you should, what you are allergic to, and what flavors do not agree with you. It's not for me to decide that you should have an appetizer first followed by the salad!

Shucks, where I come from aperitif is what comes first, then light appetizers, then soup and so on.

No Time To Waste

This is not one style fits all type of a recipe book. Rather, you must know yourself well enough or at least be willing to start to learn about yourself well enough to use this book to its full potential.

You may decide that you want to explore your cultural background more, so that may be your starting point, however Bob might want to focus on his fears that keep preventing him to achieve his heart's desire.

That doesn't mean that other ingredients are not important. But it does mean that we may start at different points in this book, and in life, and work our way around as we see it fit, which trains you in another absolutely key ingredient of success, that you must practice with tenacity: decision making!

If you're going to be successful, you must acknowledge that you are responsible for yourself and your success. You must realize that as a successful person, you must make a decision as to how your life will run and how your day will turn out!

This book makes a perfect way to practice your decision-making skills: choosing which ingredients to focus on and which ones to add a bit later and how much.

I believe that daily affirmations are something you should read well, daily. The reason for it is that we all have accumulated a gunk of bad stuff... the not-so-nice beliefs and values that beat us down as oppose to build us up. Everything else, structure it in the way that supports your beautiful being.

As you start incorporating these into your life, you will notice some very powerful and wonderful changes happening on rather consistent basis, including you becoming much more successful, confident, and happy.

As you become much more successful, please make sure that you share your success with others, me included. With today's social media being the norm, I feel certain you'll be able to find me. I get so excited when people's lives turn out for the better and when people start loving themselves and their lives.

Well, let's get started then… no time to waste!

"Life likes to be taken by the lapel and told 'I'm with you kid. Let's go!'"

Maya Angelou

1

Affirmations

What Successful People Do Daily

For a while now, I have had mentors from all walks of life and in different aspects of personal and business success. In my interactions with and observations of them, I have uncovered some remarkable similarities in their daily practices.

On a first glance, it appears that they all must have read the same book or had the same teacher, but that is not true. Many of them never crossed paths nor knew of each other.

Yet, they all seemed to have a practice of building themselves up on daily basis.

How interesting, I thought and decided to dive further into their actions to better understand this, at that time, strange practice.

How Our Brains Work

Our brains are extremely powerful and truly amazing. The world of science is yet to figure out all of the possibilities human brains are capable.

What I find incredibly fascinating is that our brains cannot tell a difference between a make-believe or play-pretend and a "reality".

Why "reality" instead of reality?

What we call "reality" is nothing more than a mere version of what's actually happened. We sort, sift, and separate through our preset filters the information that is around us on consistent basis. There is so much data produced every millisecond around us, that our brains simply cannot deliver all of that to us.

The police officers have already figured out that during the investigation they must talk to every witness possible. There can be twenty witnesses seeing the exact same event happen, yet there will be twenty different stories. There will be some similarities and trends in all of them, of course, but some of the details will be incredibly different.

Akin to a computer that when many programs are trying to run simultaneously and the computer crashes, our brains would have the exact same happen to them if every ounce of data was fully processed on the conscious level.

Our brains allow us to consciously process only so much information, at any one given time, and because there are millions of information bits that happen each second, we tend to delete, generalize, or simply ignore about 98% of it all.

Our brains, through previous inputs, decide what 2% of data is actually important that can pass all the filters and finally reach out.

But how do these inputs get into our brains and who provides the information for our super-computer?

That is an excellent question to ask!

Most of the programs that are running in our brains have been installed in our childhood.

Wait, WHAT?

Oh, yeah!

No way!

Way!

Have you ever considered that your thoughts are not yours? That your beliefs are not yours? That all of that was installed into you at your youngest and most vulnerable age and that you are consistently installing the information through radio and television programming?

It is called programming for a reason!

Vladimir Lenin understood that young minds are incredibly pliable and soak up information like sponges. This is why he famously proclaimed: "Give me four years to teach the children and the seed I have sown will never be uprooted."

The information programmed into us at that age becomes as part of us as our fingers or toes and wherever we go, that information goes. And often, left unchecked the program runs for as long as we do.

This is another reason why modern education is mostly based on teaching the children to memorize as it makes it much easier to engrain the teaching to become part of us.

Because of how the programming works and how education is designed, individuals growing up in different countries will have different "opinions" on hot topics: is socialism good or bad, nationalizing healthcare is good or bad, and so on.

How We Learn

The scientists have proven now that when we hear, read, see, or do certain things repeatedly, we start believing those to be true, regardless whether they are.

Think of commercials and stories that are repeated on the TV or other media. Or reflect on what happened during the Nazi Germany and how once peaceful people started to believe that they were somehow of the superior or submissive race.

Loud speakers were often used in the country to proclaim the Arians to be better and the same type of loud speaker was used in ghettos and concentration campus to break down the will of the people, German leadership at the time, deemed undesirable.

Once our brains accept these stories to be true and they have been programmed into your brain, your brain will only process those bits of information that agree with the original programming.

I am going to repeat what I just wrote because it is that important for you to understand:

Once your brain accepts the stories programmed into the brain as the truth, it will process only those bits of information that agree and further support the original programming.

That it why it is so important that you watch what goes into your brain and what goes into your children's brains.

The Good And
The Bad News

To help you put what I've said into perspective, think about it in terms of cars.

Say you're looking to buy a car and you've already decided that an SUV is what you want. You're not going to bother yourself with going into a sports cars only dealership or browse mini-vans on a website, as they have absolutely nothing to offer to you. You are in the business of purchasing an SUV and your sole focus is going to websites and dealerships that have SUVs for sale.

The brain processes things on a conscious and subconscious level very much the dame. This is both great and not-so-great news, depending how you'd like to look at it.

On one hand, if you're happy with what you have and where you are in life, including your attitude, health, wealth, relationships, spirituality, etc, chances are really good that you'll continue to accumulate your good fortune.

On the other hand, if you're not happy about particular things and you focus on not being happy about them, you'll continue to accumulate them and continue to be unhappy about it.

Now, I've just shared the most important aspect of this whole book right there.

Did you see it?

Well, in case you missed it, let me repeat it again: whether you're happy or not happy about what you have and where you are in life, you'll continue to get more of what you focus on!

WOW!

We get more of what we are looking for, regardless whether we are looking at it because we want it and are happy about or because we don't want it and are unhappy about it.

So, is this good news or bad news?

This is great news!

Now that you know how the darn thing works you can play the game.

Not only can you train yourself to focus on what you want (*hint: another* nugget) but you can also start changing the record, which is, very much like the loudspeakers, consistently playing between your ears, into the music you actually want to listen to and the one that is supportive of you.

You can change your story!

Go ahead and say it: "WOW!" and make sure you have a huge grin on your face, as we, my friend, have discovered a timeless success formula. (Plus smiling actually helps with your brain delivering the good chemicals to you, so make sure you keep that smile on consistently.)

The Formula

If we know that our reality is the story we tell ourselves

and we know that the story is based off the filters we use to process the world around us, then we know that by changing the filters and the story, we can change our reality.

I absolutely know how insane this sounds, but people from all over the world and from all occupations are doing it and it works for them.

So, if it works for the millions of people, it works for all of my mentors and it works for yours truly, don't you think it just might, perhaps, potentially work for you as well?!

In case you decide to study this further, there are many books on quantum physics and brain science that explain how it all works in great detail.

My version is my simplistic take and distillation on the whole thing that helps me understand and empowers me to implement.

Implementation

To change the programming and the filters, start with daily affirmations of empowering thoughts and beliefs. Remember, it can be true for you now, like things you currently believe and it can also be things that you wish to believe at some point in the future.

Read them, preferably out loud and at least once a day, preferably twice a day: first thing in the morning and last thing before you go to sleep.

I understand you may feel silly at first doing this, but you're in your home, it's just you. There is no one to judge you or poke fun at you. And heck, if the dog staring makes you feel uncomfortable, kick him out of the bedroom/den/garage, shut the door, turn the music on loud and get going.

This list provided is by no means exhaustive. You can pick the ones you want and add your own. Or create a brand new list of your own.

Oh, one more thing before I hand you the sample of the affirmation, make sure you say them out loud as if you believe it wholeheartedly. Even better, do it in the childish sing-song pattern while skipping around.

Yes, it's okay to be silly and laugh at it all, yourself included.

The Affirmations

I am a divine and powerful being.

I am strong.

I am perfect just the way I am.

I am beautiful in every way.

What I don't like, I can change. What I like, I can multiply.

My slate can be as clean as I allow it to be.

To learn something, I must remember it and embrace it fully.

I must keep repeating what I want until it becomes a second nature to me.

Even the wheel follows the deeply grooved path. My

mind is the same way.

I have the power to change the grooves: fill the ones I no longer need, dig new ones that will serve me, redirect those which are too deep.

I can and I do easily overcome challenges put before me.

There are no problems in my life, only challenges that help me grow and become a person I need to be.

I was brought into this world for a purpose.

I may not know what my purpose is, but with time, I will learn it.

I will know my purpose by observing what people reach out to me for.

I will know my purpose by feeling passionate about doing it.

I will know my purpose when I am overcome with emotions by just thinking about it.

I will know my purpose by being silent in meditation and allowing my higher self to guide me.

My purpose is the reason I am here.

The reason I am here is to be of service to others.

It is my job to find out what my talents are and in what ways I can show up for others.

By knowing and understanding the difference between servitude and service, I feel confident in what I do and how I do it.

My purpose will set me free and guide me towards the ultimate fulfillment in my life.

I understand the difference between achievement and fulfillment.

To achieve, I must set objective and take action to reach them, regardless of how I feel about them.

To become fulfilled I must act from the heart and find ways to connect my heart and my head.

To be fulfilled, I will act with love and do things that make me happy.

My only limitations are those that I impose upon myself or allow others to establish for me.

I am careful what I believe and to whom I listen.

These are the statements of truth.

I am able to create the exact life that I desire.

I have power to attract the right people in my life.

Add your own…

"The moment you doubt whether you can fly, you cease for ever to be able to do it."

J.M. Barrie

2

Beliefs

To Achieve, You Must Believe

Beliefs are things we hold to be true, regardless whether

they are.

In some teachings, belief is often called faith or certainty. They are things we take for granted and know will happen for sure, even if we can't prove them can completely explain why they are true or understand them completely.

Certainties in life are things that we create in our minds to be based on historic events we have seen, read, heard, or experienced before.

For example, I know without a shadow of a doubt that tomorrow the sun will come out. I might not see it because there are clouds, but I know that it's there because I am able to see the difference between the darkness of the night and the light of the day.

Or if I take a deep breath of air in my lungs, I know that oxygen will enter in my body. I may not completely understand how it all works or why it works the way it does, I just know it does and I don't question it.

This is what we know as the concept of "once I see it, I will believe."

What the most successful people have are the unwavering beliefs in themselves and their ability to overcome any circumstance in life. It is as if they run by a different set of rules, the ones that say "I must first believe in order to see."

It is this belief system that seems to give them power to take action on things they cannot always prove or fully explain. It is this belief system that empowers them to take a step every time, even in uncertain times.

Once they believe and act on their belief, as if it is a fact they can prove, they often seem to achieve whatever they set out to do.

It is this action that sets truly successful people apart from everyone else. Their belief system and willingness to act.

Often when we witness them doing so, we call it

confidence and sometimes stupidity if we cannot fully grasp where they are going or whether their actions will prove fruitful, especially if those actions are contrary to popular beliefs.

I think of their behavior as I would about walking.

When you take a step ahead of you, you step full on, knowing that the earth beneath you will fully support your weight and not cave in.

That certainty you feel with each step is created by your belief that the earth is strong enough for your weight.

Imagine living in a world where you do not believe that the ground ahead of you can support your weight.

Would you confidently step forward like you do now and rush to get wherever it is that you're going?

Likely not.

What would most likely happen is that you would likely put your foot forward, lightly tap, feel and test and incrementally put a bit more and more of your weight until you finally feel confident enough that the spot you have chosen to place your foot is sturdy enough. Then you'd have to repeat the process for any additional steps you wish to take.

This process would likely prove very stressful and extremely time consuming – you'd never make it anywhere!

Yet, that is how we often operate when it comes to many aspects of our lives.

We test, we probe, and uncertain about our abilities and skills.

Furthermore, we tend to latch onto our past experiences when things didn't go according to plan and when we failed.

Then we run that tape over and over in our heads, beating ourselves up and we wonder why it takes us forever to achieve positive results we so desperately seem to desire.

The solution, however simple is not always easy to implement, I truly understand that. And yet, you must believe.

I am not saying blindly believe in everything and I am not saying believe everyone. What I am saying is believe in yourself.

And make sure you do so, without a shadow of a doubt...

and watch a transformation start to happen.

How To Change
Your Beliefs

To change your belief system, you need to consciously start shifting what you think.

We know from psychology that our beliefs impact our thinking. We also know that our thinking controls what we say. And we know that what we say is closely related to what we do, when we are being completely congruent.

Using logic, we can rework the process to allow for changes on the deep level.

I have ability to choose what actions I take and how I do things, yes?

I also have ability to change what words I use, what my tonality is, and how I say what it is that I am looking to say. Agreed?

Well if I can change my actions and I can change my words, wouldn't it be plausible that I can shift how I think?

And aren't the thoughts derived from my beliefs? And is it possible that implementing the fact pointed out earlier that repetitive action, reading, hearing, and thinking can change the very nature of our brains, I am thus able to shift my beliefs.

Sure, all of these might require some work, conscious training, being present in my life, but it is all possible.

Well, if it's possible, that means I have the power to shift my beliefs from limiting ones to the thoughts and beliefs that are supportive in what it is that I am looking to achieve.

Listed below are some powerful beliefs that I have incorporated into my life that I think you may find useful to get you started on your journey.

I am given an independent mind to think freely and interpret the world in my own way.

I have a choice of how I perceive things.

I can choose what I believe and when.

I choose supporting beliefs that will carry me further not hold me behind.

As I grow and learn, I can take up new beliefs that are supportive of whole me.

We all do the best we can with the information we have at the time. (This particular statement can do wonders to help you forgive yourself and others for all of the past actions.)

I can let go of non-supportive beliefs easily when I decide to do so.

I know with certainty that what I truly believe and what I can see in my mind's eye, I can achieve.

You can add your own beliefs you currently have or wish to have that are supportive of whole you:

To create space for your newly founded empowering beliefs, write down some beliefs that no longer serve you, that you wish to let go:

To let go of the old beliefs, take a moment to read what you have written down.

Take a deep breath, hold for few seconds and then blow it out through your mouth (feel free to make a sound if needed).

Repeat few times until you feel comfortable and relaxed.

Read them over calmly and think about what those beliefs have done for you.

Maybe they held you back from being a person you know you can be.

Maybe you have been harboring some negative feelings about some event or person in the past because of those beliefs.

Have those beliefs served you well or have they kept you unhappy and bitter?

Are you ready and willing to let go of these non-supportive and negative beliefs now?

If you answered "yes", then take another look at them, take a deep breath, hold for count of 3, and then blow it out through your mouth (feel free to add a sigh or sound).

Then state:

"These are beliefs I have held before that no longer serve me. I choose to let them go now. I no longer need them."

Then, take a deep breath in again and blow it out through your mouth. As you breathe out, visualize the burden leaving your body.

Repeat as often as needed until you feel lighter.

Then, gently thank yourself for allowing yourself to get rid of old and useless stuff and congratulate yourself on taking in new, supporting beliefs.

"Reality is merely an illusion, albeit a persistent one."

Albert Einstein

3

My Story

What Is Real

What is reality?

Often, we hear others say things like "keep it real.", but what does that actually mean?

While, of course, I understand the cultural connotations around the sentence, people looking for truth and grounding

story, I have come to realize that reality is nothing more but a story I tell myself.

Events in our lives happen all the time and those are nothing more but events. However, we tend to attach meanings to events that happen to us and we often do it so that we can figure out how to reach to those things.

In a wonderful book, "Obstacles Is The Way", Ryan Holiday reminds us that nothing has a meaning but for the meaning we give it through sharing some incredibly powerful stories.

An event is only an event. It's not good nor bad; it is how we interpret the said event that makes it either good or bad.

But how can it be so?

It is quite simple. To illustrate this, I will use an example from a financial market.

In 2008 the financial world nearly collapsed as we know it. There are many books, movies, and stories of people losing everything and then some. Many of those that lost everything, 2008 and the financial tsunami that occurred are likely bad events that have transpired in their lives.

There are those who have profited handsomely from the same events that have occurred, making them millions of dollars or more. Many of them will swear that events surrounding the 2008 market crash was the absolute best time ever.

So, how is it possible that the exact same event can be the most horrific thing that happened and the most amazing thing that happened at the same time?

Understanding that event is just an event and it's how you look at it that makes it either good or bad is how you can explain this phenomenon.

But wait Nev… does this mean that I can actually change what the event is and can change it from good to bad and from bad to good by simply attaching different meanings for the event???

That is EXACTLY what I'm saying!

Situation is NEVER the problem, it's how you interpret it.

Problems Are
Necessary

We often refer to challenges and situations as problems when they are something we do not desire. Otherwise, as Tony Robbins says, we call them "surprises" and we *love those.*

Consider this, every challenge and every situation, has an appropriate solution. Often, that solution is imbedded in the circumstances of the challenge or situation itself.

Furthermore, in order to feel good about ourselves we have to have achieved something and we do that by solving a, you guessed it, problem.

My mentor, Joel Bauer, often shares a story of how he taught Dali Lama how Problems = Happiness.

He says that by having problems we have to search for solutions, which gives us purpose. By finding appropriate solutions and following our purpose we feel satisfied and fulfilled, confident and determined and that leads to happiness. However, happiness is a fleeting emotion and to continue to have happiness in life, we must continue to be satisfied with solutions to the problems by following our purpose.

As such:

Problems = Happiness

Next time a problem comes up in your life, think of this equation and get super excited. If you solve it, you'll be happy. If you don't, you will have a purpose which will also make you happy. Either way, HAPPY!

What's Your Story?

Following my mentor's logic, I have concluded that if I can choose how to interpret everything and my interpretation is my story, then I can choose to assign supporting beliefs and interpret situations in a way that makes me happy and moving closer to my ultimate goals.

Because of my teaching I interact with many people from all over the world. Often, I hear folks come up with stories they carry with themselves that are clearly not supportive, yet they clutch onto them as if they have stumbled onto a pile of pure gold.

When I see people like that, I can't help myself but to think of a Discovery Channel show I once saw as a teenager.

There are these monkeys, in Africa, I believe, that live in a predominantly desert location. Food and water can be scarce and so the natives have figured out an easy way to catch a monkey.

I think they were catching them for food, but for my teenage brain that was too much to deal with, so my smart brain simply deleted over that piece of information.

What I do recall is the exact methodology to catch the monkeys.

In a large hollowed tree trunk, the hunters will place a small piece of fruit and drill a tiny hole. A hole so small that the monkey will be able to put its empty paw in, but once it's clenched into a fist the hole is to small to pull out of and the trunk is too heavy to carry.

The monkeys would every time go to the trunk, put their hands in the hole and hold onto the fruit.

They would see the hunter approach. They would scream and shout, likely petrified of the human coming every so closer. They would jump, try to pull the log, try to chew around the arm.

I mean they did just about everything, except ONE THING that would have made all the difference in the world, let go of the fruit and run free.

Instead, the animal viciously holds onto one thing it will never have and dies as a result of it.

That is exactly what I think of when I hear a story of why someone cannot have everything they desire in their life and those monkeys are exactly who I think about when I ask people to let go of the story and they exclaim "I can't!"

I guess us and the primates are not that far off quite yet.

What the human likely should have said, but didn't is "I don't want to." But that would be admitting to the fact that the stupid story they lug with themselves for years is what is preventing them from soaring.

In the hopes that I can help you stop being the monkey that is about to become someone's dinner, I'd like for you to ponder this:

As I have an independent mind to think freely, I can choose my thoughts and as earlier pointed out my beliefs.

If I can choose my thoughts, which lead me to experience the world through the sense of feeling, that means I can choose my feelings too.

My feelings are expressed through a range of emotion (as one of the mentors said "an energy in motion") and because of my ability to make many choices, I have a power to decide how to express and when to release my emotions.

This alone has helped me a great deal manage my bursts of emotional expressions. Until learning this and practicing it consistently, I experience a lot of anger and my emotional reaction to many things was incredibly powerful – sadly not in the good way.

So, if I can use this to help me shift in a way that people that have known me for years, can barely recognize me, chances are pretty darn good, you too can do it.

Some of the emotions that we tend to express come from, yet again our childhood.

You see, we might be a wee bit taller and a wee bit heavier, but we are those same children we were years ago and left unchecked, we run the same patterns in our beliefs, thinking and emotions we did as toddlers!

YIKES!

Once I realized that some emotions I carried and expressed we only a crutch, something I used as a child to get what I wanted and express dissatisfaction with results I was receiving, I was able to empower myself to shift my responses.

Friends, family, and co-workers were instrumental in my shift as I became much more aware how I was leaving them with my reactions.

Tantrums are never pleasant nor welcome events, even when they come from a toddler. But they are even more some detrimental to all when they are delivered from an adult.

But how do you know that your emotional response to something has turned into a tantrum?

Consider being present and paying attention to how you reach when something happens and how others react to you afterwards. If you are in a meeting and your response leaves the room silent or everyone around you change their body posture and they shut down, chances are you have just delivered a temper tantrum, tampering all of the creativity and collaboration in the room.

If that is exactly what you wanted to accomplish, great work you did it.

But on an off chance that you did not want to shut everyone down, perhaps a shift in your response and your reaction is required.

Oftentimes the non-supporting emotions, thoughts, feelings and reactions are still with you because you use them to support your story. Yeah, that very piece of fruit that is about to kill you.

Your story can be supportive or non-supportive. And which one you run is entirely your choice.

When I choose to tell myself the non-supportive story, I am using it as a crutch, as an excuse, as a 100-ton rucksack on my back that literally prevents me from achieving what I ultimately know is my purpose and destiny. The non-supporting story is the excuse of why I let myself down.

Habits

Often a question in educational setting is posed of how long it takes to create a habit or get rid of it and replace it with new one.

People will throw all kinds of numbers and for some reason there is a story that is widely accepted into a belief that it takes 21 days to do so.

For someone who likes to get into specifics and asks "When you say 21 days, do you mean, 21 24-hour cycles?" Often that shuts the presenter down and I'm seen as a rebel trying to throw them off. I'm not. I just want to understand what they mean.

Is it 21 consecutive days? Do weekends count? Can I take a break in the meantime? What does it all mean?

21 days! What a load of baloney!

You can instantaneously create habits and destroy them, just like you can thoughts and beliefs. It takes but a mere second. It takes but a mere decisions to shift.

Don't believe me?

Let's try this test on for a size!

Let's assume that you're single. You have your daily routines; people you spend time with and things you enjoy doing. You have your favorite outfits, habits, and routines. They are as part of you and you are of them.

One day, your eye catches an eye of another and next thing you know BAM, you're in love.

You change your entire routine, you have time for this person, no matter what. You change they way you dress and start eating foods you never ate before. Your entire world has changed because well they happen to like…

How long did it take you to change? A moment! You didn't wait 21 days, you just changed.

So if you can change when in love with someone else, you can change when in love with the new habit, new results, new you. And it only takes as long as you make a decision to change.

If I wanted, I can choose today, right this moment, to let go of all my non-supportive stories and replace them with the supportive ones. The challenge I have often encountered with doing so, is that oftentimes the story was part of my identity, the way I perceived myself.

It wasn't that I was always happy with my story or that it made me feel good. It's that it would become my reason as to why I could or worse yet, couldn't do something. Maybe you can relate:

I'm too small to play rugby.
I didn't get that job because of my last name.
They did not choose my presentation because I'm a guy.
I can't start my own business, because I am too young.
Nobody will listen to me because I an accent.

All of those are excuses. They are a story for when things don't go our way. They are a story will tell ourselves to give ourselves a permission to give up before we even get started, before even taking action.

I shared my baggage. Your turn now.

What story (or stories) have you been telling yourself that have prevented you from achieving your goals and reaching your higher purpose?

What stories would your higher self tell you to support your life's purpose?

"Ninety-nine percent of the failures come from people who have the habit of making excuses."

George Washington Carver

4

Reasons Or Results

Excuses

Oh, we are incredible telling ourselves stories to give ourselves an out. Those stories are simply excuses, nothing more, nothing less.

A mentor years ago told me that I can have one of two

things: a reason or a result. The choice was totally up to me.

"If you create results, you never go looking for reasons. You don't need them, your results speak louder than any words you can muster. But the moment you don't get results, you start running reasons. It's bad enough that you're providing all these reasons, all these excuses to those that depended on you. But now you start telling those reasons to yourself. The poor, sad, woe-is-me story to yourself and then you believe it!" he continued.

Oh, how heartless! What an awful, awful man!

Yet, he's right.

In my almost century of life, I have never heard someone provide reasons when they achieved results. Accolades maybe, but never reasons or excuses.

I am yet to hear a winning team share a sob story how the gym was flooded and they couldn't work out. How alarm clock ran out of batteries, how traffic was horrid or how their boss is a jerk.

If they shared such a story, it was more of a story of a triumph how even with such odds they succeeded. How gym was flooded and they went to train in a park. How they set 3 alarm clocks for a meeting as to not miss it. How they left 2 hours early to ensure traffic would not impede and how a jerk of a boss was won over by a winning strategy even he or she could not say no to.

It boils down to two words REASONS or RESULTS.

Learning those lessons were crucially important to me and my success and those are the same lessons and words that I run by my students, coaching clients, and even my own family and friends.

I am not interested in your reasons, so don't even start.

Every day I decide to take action or to not take action, which too is an action of a kind, just passive one that does not support me.

If I know that I can ultimately have reasons or results, I have to make a decision which of the two I wish to have.

Personally, I like to have results. Because when I have the results, I don't need reasons. And frankly, it's embarrassing to have to explain yourself. To avoid the embarrassment, I take action.

Does that mean that I achieve my objective every time, without a fault?

I wish I could say yes. But, no, I don't. There are times that I miss my goal.

But, due to this powerful lesson, instead of providing excuses for failure, I apologize to those that depended on me and I learn from my omissions.

This disempowers my ability to give myself an out. It acknowledges to others that I have let them down and it gives me permission to learn and grow, so that I can see what I didn't see before to ensure the same mistake does not happen again.

What reasons have you used in the past when you weren't successful?

What is your plan to prevent having to provide reasons but rather show results?

The Self-Fulfilling Prophecy

When I decide to do something, I do whatever it takes to get it done.

Most of us are incredibly weak in spirit. We say yes even when we don't mean it, for the fear of rejection of what others will think of us.

Because the "yes" was so weak and not sincere, we tend to back down often before we get started and nearly always when the going gets tough.

As we've learned by now, the lack of results means we must provide the reasons, so we do. We come up with excuses for others, but most often for ourselves, which kills our spirit and weakens our "yes" even further.

So, what is the solution?

Say no more often.

Tim Ferris in one of the interviews asked a guest how he makes a decision on what projects and investments to take on. The response was so shocking and so powerful that it burned in my memory.

"If it's not a H*LL YES, it's a NO." the guest simply replied.

Think about it. We say yes to too many things and make commitments all the time we end up breaking.

Sure, you create this aura around you that you cannot keep your word. But what is worse is that inability to keep your word is what is killing your spirit from the inside.

By deciding to participate only in events, businesses, investments, gatherings, and so on, that truly excite you, you dwindle down on a myriad of things that are presented in your life as an option.

Long time ago I learned that people don't get disappointed in a firm NO. They do get deeply disappointed in a flimsy YES.

When you say YES to someone, they act as if whatever you have agreed to will happen. When you don't show up, it's a huge disappointment, until of course you do it so often they quickly learn that your yes is more of a maybe than anything else.

The flimsy yes is why most businesses fail. The flimsy yes is why well over 50% of marriages fail. The flimsy yes is a reason why you have those success-detrimental stories about yourself.

As Bob Newhart said in his popular comedy show video: "STOP IT."

Start being much more discriminating in what you agree to. Sure, it will be awkward at first, but soon it will make a lot of sense and it will simplify your life.

What's more, if will build your credibility, your spirit and your commitment level.

Once you say YES to something, make sure you commit to it all the way and see it until it's finished.

Take a new mantra into your life that says: There is no giving up and there is no walking away. Create an environment where the boats are burned and you can't turn away.

Then, follow the process of act, breathe, act, breathe, act, breathe... it's one step, one task, one move, one lift, at a time.

But the key is to keep going, keep showing up, and never giving up.

Before you know it, you will start creating a brand new you. The you that is committed, concentrated, reliable, and above all one that others and you can count on.

Pain

Long time ago, I have learned a powerful lesson that life is about making up your mind and then doing it. Yet, often we stop because of the pain and fear. Let's address those in a very logical way of thinking.

What is pain?

I am not talking about the physical discomfort that we sometimes experience here. Although, the medical professionals will tell you that feeling pain is a good thing. Why? Simply because pain is a symptom of something not functioning well in our bodies and it is the nature's way to let us know that we have done something or that something is happening within us that needs to be fixed in order to save our lives.

Funny how nature is so intuitive.

The pain I would like to focus here is more of the mental and emotional discomfort that often arises from doing something that a) we shouldn't have done, b) we have never done before – energy utilization to shift from static to motion (remember the physics lesson about things in motion and what it takes to stop them), c) we perceive will happen or be required to achieve what we're looking to do.

Emotional pain we experience from things we shouldn't have done is a great educator. It allows us to put energy out to others and see what results we collect back. If the result causes pain, that is a good thing. It is letting you know that you should not do whatever you did again and not in the way and with the people you did it with.

That doesn't mean don't do that ever. It simply means don't do it in that exact way, time, location, and surrounding.

The two other kinds of emotional pains are the ones that get us stuck most often and I find that the two often run parallel with each other.

The human beings are inherently extremely lazy and the mere thought of having to exert energy into doing something you've never done before appears rather unappealing. We too follow the principles of physics and find it much easier to keep moving if we are already moving and find it much easier to stand still if we are in that state already.

Where we often find ourselves is in the state of static and

the thought of having to move and expand energy in the process is the pain we perceive, which is why we get stopped well before we even get started.

Think about it. Have you ever sat on the couch and thought to yourself "I should go work out." Then the following thoughts and questions likely entered your brain: as soon as the show is over; oh, it's raining right now; it's too cold/hot to go now; look at the time, it will be packed in the gym at this hour; I guess I could, but then I'd have to get up, get dressed, get into my car; I don't know where my gym shoes are… and so on.

Pain is only what we tell ourselves and often it's used to prevent us from doing things. It is simply a mental game we play with ourselves that gives us an excuse of why we don't need to or can't or shouldn't do something.

The way I see it, you will feel the pain, period. Just know that, accept it, and move on.

You can feel the pain now and do it, or you can sit back and feel pain later. The choice is entirely yours, but please know, pain is here and always will be.

Some time ago, I went to San Diego to read, write, find balance, reconnect, and rejuvenate. They have a beautiful story in Hawaii, that we come from the sea and that when you're out of balance, out of whack, you must enter the Ocean in order to be re-energized and re-balanced so that you stay connected to your true (higher) self and of course to the planet. Some people will call this grounding and have different ways to achieve it.

I believe that going to the water and to the nature to be true for me, so I wanted to go into the ocean and just let go (plus it's fun to jump in the waves).

I walked to the ocean, the wave came in, and water was to my ankles. I winced in pain, as the water was very chilly (I checked the report and it was about 60 degrees).

As the cold water hit me, my wish to go into the ocean changed, in an instant. I started rationalizing as to why I shouldn't go in, "It's too cold. I don't really need to go in. What am I trying to prove? This is insane. I can just meditate and enjoy the breeze. What if I catch a cold and get sick? This is not worth it…"

My mother called me, I was telling her about my experience, and she too supported my pain process of not going into the water, "there'll be next time. You don't need to go in, just because it's there…"

As I was looking to the ocean, I noticed that all of the surfers had wetsuits on, however there were about 5 swimmers or so jumping in the waves and laughing. They looked like they had a good time.

Then it hit me: pain is only what we perceive in our heads to prevent us from doing what's difficult at the time.

Pain is to prevent the change as we like things to stay the same and predictable, it gives us certainty. I also noticed that for those that perceive fun in the chilly water being more worth than the pain of adjusting to the water temperature are the ones who went in even though they were cold, you could see it on their faces and body language.

Right then and there I decided to go for it.

I made up my mind and started walking. To be honest, I wasn't walking as quickly as my ego would like to admit, but I was moving forward. I was determined to have fun in the ocean. Once I was in the water, my body adjusted to the temperature change rather quickly and I had a blast. I was smiling and I laughing when the wave would splash me, I went over and under, I body surfed. It was amazing and I am very happy I endured a short-term pain for years of great memories.

Since then, I learned of the cold-water immersion being incredibly good for our bodies (please consult your medical practitioner because just as it can be beneficial to healthy individuals it can be deadly for weakened immune systems and bodies). I have also realized very quickly that cold water emersion (lake, ocean, bath or shower) can not only improve how our bodies function, it also does a miracle with training of the brain and the will power. It helps put both the physical and mental pain in the proper perspective and it appears to be used by many high performing individuals.

I have been a regular practitioner of the ritual and use it on nearly daily basis. Again, in the spirit of full disclosure, I do find it rather challenging to do it in the dead of winter, when my house is cool and outside is plenty cold, but I make myself experience it, even if it is for 10 seconds only.

My past events have taught me a few important concepts I would like to leave you with to meditate on.

Pain is short-term; the lesson it carries is eternal.

If I only focus on the pain and shut down the lesson, I would have wasted a great opportunity.

When you realize that the result is greater than the pain of starting, it is easy to "just go for it".

Having a vision of what certain action can do and making it so vivid, so powerful, so enticing, will help you get over the initial pain of taking action.

Make up your mind and do it.

Take a small step towards what it is that you want and are looking to create. The size of the step doesn't matter. What matters is that action is taken, consistently and that you get yourself in motion. Then, the physics will take care of the rest and motion and action taking will be the new normal.

Allow yourself time to adjust to the change, but don't give in to the pain urges.

Taking a pause to give yourself time to acknowledge the pain and to adjust to the new is okay and perfectly fine. Just be aware of the trap that if you stay in the "pause" too long, you may never proceed any further, so make sure it's a very brief one.

In the next chapter, we will talk about change and how to create it in your life. But for now, it's your turn to reflect on pain and what is has done for you thus far.

How has pain stopped you from achieving something you wanted in the past?

Have you ever used the pain to help you make a change and shift towards something you wanted?

What was that and how did it happen?

What pain do you perceive in reaching your goals?

What is your plan to overcome your pain and achieve what it is that you desire?

"The secret to change is to focus all of your energy not on fighting the old, but on building the new."

Socrates

5

Change

As a child I didn't care much for physics or history, for that matter. But it wasn't the subject itself that was boring, rather the delivery method of those teaching me. As an adult, I am fascinated with both and every chance I get, I dive deeper into the subjects as history teaches us important lessons we can all learn and physics provides the basics for understanding life.

Physics is very clear on energy and the fact that each and every single one of is nothing more than a body of electricity walking around.

An important law of physics that I'd like to help you recall is the one the is very clear about energy:

1. Everything is one thing and that is energy.
2. Energy cannot be created nor destroyed, it can only change form.
3. Energy must be acted upon to change form.

The basic laws of energy and gravity shapeshift our lives and govern everything around us. If that is all true, then it must be true that our thoughts are energy as well. And if so, they can change form.

It also must be true that our feelings are energy too and that there is an action that is required for those emotions to be shifted. Emotion – energy in motion.

Whether I do something or not, I am taking action. Even non-acting is an action of a kind, a force. To keep my thoughts and emotions at a stand-still I keep taking the same action or lack thereof.

Action I take can help me manifest the energy of my thoughts and feelings into something tangible – another form of energy. These will be my results.

This means that when there are certain beliefs we hold on a particular matter, those manifest themselves into thoughts, whether what you silently think or audibly say. Actions we take then lead into particular results.

Edison, it is said, has failed well over 10,000 times in attempting to create a light bulb. However, when asked, Edison himself has stated that he's never failed, not even once. He successfully proved 10,000 ways of how a light bulb cannot be created.

In following his example, it is easy to conclude that there is no such thing as failure in life, only results.

Whenever you take an action, there will be a result at the end of that equation. You or I may not always get results that we were looking for, but those can be changed by the changing the actions we take.

So, to be successful, all we have to do is take action and look at the results we are getting. If those are not to our liking, we must change the action taken. Eventually we will reach the results we desire.

For example, say that you want to have a body of a Greek God, or demi-god if you're not shooting for the ultimate result. While yes, there are some that are gifted with special genes of just looking that way without much work, majority of us must do something about it. Most of us cannot sit on the couch for 10 hours a day, drink case of beer a day and gorge on every single cake and doughnut that comes our way. We'd likely have to change what we eat, how long we sit and do nothing, how often we work out and what types of activities we are taking. That is all action my friend.

Sure, you can go for a plastic surgery, a liposuction but that too is taking action and requiring some energy expenditure on your end.

Bottom line is, if you want for something to change, you must change. You must take action before a you receive a different result.

Once you get the results you want, then you must keep doing the same thing consistently to keep getting the same results.

In keeping with our working out analogy, I can't go to gym once and expect my physique to change. I can't say not to one doughnut and expect that all of a sudden my body will change. I must work out consistently, I must eat well and saying no to those sweetly treats on a very consistent basis.

Einstein is quoted to have said that definition of insanity is doing the same thing over and over again expecting a different result. In keeping with his philosophy, I cannot keep doing the same thing over and over and expect different results. It simply does not work.

So how much change should I exert?

Many people think that they must take a giant leap or make one big move. In following successful people, it appears that the secret lies in small things.

Going back to physics, we know that only one degree in water temperature is what is needed and all the difference between simply boiling water and creating steam to power a locomotive. One, tiny degree!

So, focus on one small thing you do every day. Like the turtle in the story, consistent action beats one big action every time.

Speaking of power of one, it appears that one degree change in the flight plan of a plane early on in the flight will result in arriving to New York or Miami.

Someone once told me that a plane leaving Los Angeles towards New York is 99% of the time on the wrong path, however the plane and the pilots constantly monitor the changes and adjust the course ever so slightly and often, that plane ends up in New York and not in Miami!

What I'm saying here is to really focus on small incremental changes on daily basis. Over the course of the year, that can make all the difference that there is.

Most baseball enthusiasts know that the greatest baseball players strike on 6 out of 7 balls. Sadly in schools we are taught that this would be failing. In sports, and often in life, what makes the great, well Great, is that one home run that changes the result of the game.

So, don't be afraid to step up to bat and don't get discouraged to strike out. Remember, all you need is that one homerun to make all the difference and make you a success.

What are some small daily changes you can make starting right now to bring you closer to your goal?

What are some of the changes that you have implemented in the past?

Why did it work for you? What is it that made it stick?

Acceptance

The greatest leaders we look upon with admiration have done a lot of things that many of us would find repulsive, unethical, immoral, etc. However, they have also done a few things (sometimes only one thing) that is good and beneficial to the humanity as a whole and as such they are remembered for the good they have provided us.

Now don't use this as an excuse to act poorly. I use it to inspire me to know that even though there may be things that I have done wrong, if I am willing to learn and grow from it and I'm willing to do good for the humanity, that I will be ultimately accepted.

Accept people for who they are, with all their faults, but

challenge their behavior when unacceptable

Accept yourself for all that you are and don't be afraid to challenge your behavior and change it to fit you better to a person you want to be.

Learn to love yourself. Once you do that, you will stop the madness of chasing others to accept and love you in order to feel the emotion of love.

I could write a whole book on acceptance and love, but this book is simply not it. I just want to challenge and encourage you to truthfully look at yourself and find love and peace within, not outside you.

I hate it when someone says "you complete me." That's stupid. Others cannot complete you. You must find a way to complete yourself within you in order to live independently and not co-dependently.

You cannot love others until you learn to love yourself.

You cannot be happy and hate or are discontent with parts or all of who you are.

Because of the self-hate, you will treat others who remind you of what you hate within yourself with disrespect, fostering the negative emotions.

Think of that next time someone makes you uncomfortable. What is it that they had said or did that made you feel that way? Question more!

If there are pieces of yourself you don't like, work to change them or find beauty in them. It is rather hard to hate what you admire and find beautiful, so find beauty in all that you are.

There are no perfections and no mistakes, only lessons and ability to progress and improve.

When connecting with people, don't look at it from the perspective of what they can do for you, rather see what you can help them with. Start with service, but not with servitude, as two are very different.

Ask others "how may I serve you best" and be sincere about your service to them, without ever looking for what you can get out of it.

What are the things you'd love to love about you?

Growth

Grow or Die,
The Choice Is Entirely Yours

Biology and nature are all around us. While, I'm sure by now, you are thinking this is high school in a book, please consider if I'm wrong.

Following the way of the nature and considering biology we get a great lesson in life and success.

In order to live, I must grow. When I stop moving and stop growing, I start dying.

Consider a tree, if you will. It does not think. It has no limits or emotions. The sun shines, the rain falls, and the little seed has everything required to live.

It doesn't plan to grow only a foot tall. It does not plan to end someone's table or a shelf. It only grows and grows as high as it possibly can and it lives as long as it possibly can.

So why do we humans think we are different? Why do we give ourselves only a foot of growth or limited lifespan? Why not grow as high as we can and plan to live as long as we can. Even though we all know it must end someday, why not plan to give it our all until the very last breath?

There is a great quote I recall from H.S. Thompson that says:

Life should not be a journey to the grave with the intention of

arriving safely in a pretty and well-preserved body, but rather to skid in broadside in a cloud of smoke, thoroughly used up, totally worn out, and loudly proclaiming "Wow! What a Ride!

I think of it often whenever I believe I'm playing too safe. Life is meant to be lived, fully. Enjoyed, fully. Experienced, fully.

Universe is filled with infinite possibilities. To experience them, I must stay open to them and to receiving them.

To change my results, I must change my action. To change my action, I must change my feelings and my thoughts. To change my thoughts I must seek new teachings and experiences, I must continue to learn, to grow. And if I don't know where to start, finding a great mentor to get me there, is a good idea.

The perceived difficulty of challenges in my life are in direct proportion with my personal growth. If I'm a level 3 person and I have an obstacle at level 6, I will say "that's a big problem, I cannot solve it." If, however I grow, learn, and become a level 8 person, the same level 6 obstacle will feel insignificant.

To help you illustrate my point, think of learning how to do something for the first time. You're very uncertain, possibly untrusting, paying attention to the smallest detail, sweating, focused, etc. You might have even not been able to achieve the set outcome first 5, 10, 20 times. But once you learned how to do it and became very confident doing so, it became automatic.

Not only could you do it very quickly and very accurately, you could probably do other tasks while doing it.

Never, ever give up! Once you find something that you're passionate about, your purpose for being here, your life's mission, don't give up.

If you are surrounded by people who doubt you, you have 3 options:

1) Find a different group of people
2) Stop telling them your dreams
3) Use their energy to fuel yours. Prove them wrong and make them eat their words.

There is no set time when you will achieve what you've set out to achieve. It will happen you just must keep at it. It doesn't matter how long you have been at it. It doesn't matter how many times you have reached unwanted outcome.

A mentor of mine says goals are stupid. At first I wasn't quite sure I agreed, but now I think I understand.

What is the point of setting a date to accomplish something big and missing it? So you're off by a week or a few months or even a few years. WHO CARES!

As long as you don't give up and keep pushing forward time is irrelevant. So he ways, don't have goals, have objectives, have missions. And then, of course, keep at it every day!

Do you have the number of times or years (maybe even months) you're willing to do some things for and then when it doesn't go the way you want it to, you quit?

To help you go past that point, think of a baby learning to walk. They get up, then fall down, get up, fall down... up, down, up, down... for months!!!

Go squat for months and see what happens! I bet majority of you won't even try. A handful will and will give up in the first hour or less. And there may be one or two truly outgoing folks who will keep at it.

They, my friends, will have the buns of steel and a mind so sharp, so focused that they can change the world in an instant.

But, I digress...

Now imagine being that baby's parent. You watch them go up and fall, up and fall, up and fall.

How many times will you allow the baby to go up and down before you tell the child to give up and tell them it's not worth it?

Will you say "honey, you've tried for 2 months straight and it's not working. Maybe walking is just not for you. It's okay baby, you don't need to walk. Just crawl for the rest of your life. People will understand."

NO!

You keep encouraging the baby, you clap, you say "good job. Keep up. Come on. You can do it."

You keep smiling. You are shaking their favorite bottle on your end enticing them to come. You are doing anything and everything you can possibly think of to help them onto their feet and once they figure it out, BOOM they are gone!
Now you're running all over the house after them trying to keep up.

This is the attitude you must have for yourself, your ventures, and life in general. Be your own super-awesome parent doing anything and everything to get yourself going.

In what way do you want to grow?

How specifically do you want to grow and what do you want to achieve?

What is your plan on enticing yourself to continue to go for what it is that you want?

"You cannot make progress without making decisions."

Jim Rohn

6

The Warrior Mindset

Fears

What is fear?

Fear is not real. It is just a story I tell myself. Fear is my belief of what pain I might have to endure in some point in future. Fear is the anticipation of what may happen in the future, which most often is not real nor realistic.

Once I accept that, I can move past the fear I'm feeling.

Going back to biology, you might recall that there is a part of the brain that is meant to protect us and to keep us alive. It is often called a "lizard brain" as it is the oldest part of our brain, mostly functioning on autopilot. It is the part of the brain that makes us freeze, flight, or fight in a dangerous situation. It's not a bad part of the brain (by the way stop calling things good or bad, they just simply are, ok?!) and it's truly meant to keep our race up and running into eternity.

The trouble with this part of the brain is that it perceives many things as threats and if allowed to run without filters, without control, it can absolutely make you want to run, fight, or freeze and become uncapable of doing anything.

I keep reminding myself that my mind is conditioned to protect me. It will tell me stories to keep me safe in the realm of things that I know and I'm comfortable with. It is like an overprotective mother. It means well, but does not allow for new experiences.

When I hear it speak to me – it typically shares the stories of horror and what could go wrong, I simply thank it for the input and move forward.

Now, that doesn't mean that your brain says "um dude you're on the 20th floor roof and next step there is nothing" you say "gee thanks" and go for it. Use your common sense here!

I'm mostly talking about things like I want to go out on

New Year's Eve. My brain, which was fed the fresh dose of Constant Negative News says "uhm, there are a lot of bad people out there, so you shouldn't go because if you do, you could die." While yes, there are some bad apples out there and yes, I could potentially run into them, the probability is much smaller than what my brain tells me.

The conditioned brain wants to be right. It will find supportive evidence everywhere in order to prove that it was right.

Oh, this one is very good. Quite excellent if I might say so myself.

So check this. Say you believe that women are bad drivers. Your brain has this cool feature called Reticular Activating System or RAS (not to be confused with resident advisors in your local college who are also called RAs). The RAS job is to find things that are congruent with your line of thinking and once you believe something this bad boy goes to work and scans and searches to find EXACTLY what it is that you're looking for.

So, in the case of women are bad drivers, your brain will rarely even notice a guy who should have never been allowed to even look at a vehicle none the less drive one. But it will find and record every female who makes an even smallest blunt in traffic. You will likely make an exclamation that you're right and point at the evidence, ahem the driver you just witnessed, which further confirms to RAS to keep searching for this particular thing.

Don't believe me? Pay attention next time you drive and see what happens!

In my live events I do some fun activities on the spot to showcase it right away, but no room here for that. I guess if you want to play along with me, you'll just have to come see it for yourself live.

But I digress…

When I find new beliefs, my brain will work very hard to find support for those beliefs and will find evidence everywhere around me.

When I change, my world changes.

I must take unconditional action to experience change. Often times I find myself taking action when it's convenient, when I feel like it. What I have discovered is that in order to see the massive change I was wanting, I had to take action even when I did not feel like it.

When I decided to get in shape and get, what I call, the body of the Greek God (now you know why I used this term earlier… hey I'm nothing if not consistently me) that decision had to come with unconditional action. That meant that I had to eat right and avoid fast food restaurants even when I didn't feel like it. It meant that when I was tired from working late and had a challenging day in the office, I would need to prepare nutritious food for myself or simply not eat. I had to set some serious rules for myself and follow them. It meant that when I set up that I needed to work out, I had to get off the couch, turn off TV and get busy.

Keep doing things that are challenging until they become habit.

Habit forming will take as long as it takes; there is no magic number. It's as quick as a decision you make. The stick-ability factor comes from the strength of that decision.

What fears do you have?

Have you ever done something that scared you (even as a child)? What?

How did you feel afterwards?

How do you plan to overcome my fears? What action will you take for each?

When will you take that action?

Success

It's funny that I titled the book with word "success" in it, but I only use it as a part of chapter. Why?

Well, while success has a cool ring to it and many see it as the end result, I see it as a byproduct of many other aspects that I find are much more important. I think it's important we mention it. Afterall it's in the name, but that's such a small portion of the big picture that I believe that focusing just on that would be a huge disservice to you, the reader.

Doing martial arts was the best thing I could have been involved in during my formative years. During that time, I was taught how to be a warrior.

I remember one time we showed up at the dojo and there was no power, no heat, in the dead of winter. Snow was about knee high and only about five of us showed up. It was Saturday morning training and the Sensei asked us if we would rather just go home. We unanimously decided to stay and practice.

We changed and went inside the dojo. He started with a warm up for lightly jogging in circle around the dojo and then he led us outside.

If you have ever done martial arts, then you know you practice barefoot. We followed without a question. We went into the hallway onto the cold tile and from there up the steps into the brisk morning.

Parking lot nearby was empty and he decided we run in

the knee-high snow for a few minutes before going back inside.

When I told my mother about it, she told me we were insane.

But there was a purpose for this: **when you commit to doing something, you commit in spite of anything that may come, including the cold winter morning and knee-high snow.**

It was the best practice I've ever had and it thought me a powerful lesson: I can do things that sometimes seem impossible and insane! So here is my life of warrior rules:

There is no try! There is only do or do not do.

I was taught this very important lesson in martial arts. The Sensei would show us a move or tell us to do something. Then it was up to us to do it.

One time he called me up to perform a new technique. As I was walking up, I said, "Okay, I'll try."

The look on his face I will never forget. He told me to stop and go back where I was standing.

Then he said, "In life there is no try. If you try, you failed before you even did anything! Have you ever seen a mother give a birth trying but never doing? Have you ever seen a tree only trying to grow, but not growing? It's impossible! There must be clear and distinct purpose about you and what you do. When you step up, you must make a choice: do or do not do. If you do, then you give it all you got and see yourself on the other side of achieving whatever you set out to do. And you work and you strive and you push until there is nothing left inside you. You do not give up. There is no walk away. If you chose not to do, then you go back and tell everyone and yourself all the reasons you couldn't do. But don't you ever try!"

That day I made a decision that I follow to this day. I decided to do!

Act in spite of fear.

Make a commitment and then go for it.

Show up every day and keep pressing play.

Habits are made through practice.

Each day you create stronger habits, so practice being your very best every day.

Commit to mastery.

Now is the time.

To achieve what you set out to do, you must do whatever it takes.

Failure and giving up are not an option.

Remove your conditions for taking action.

It doesn't have to be perfect.

Believe, but move your feet.

The size of your opponent (or obstacle) does not matter, the one with greater determination will always win.

Be present.

When it gets tough, just breathe, but don't stop.

When and why do you need to be a warrior in my life?

What is your warrior way? What rules do you want to embody?

Who is watching you go through life and how you operate that will likely follow in your footsteps or judge you on who you are based on what you do?

How do you want them to see you? What qualities do you want them to have?

"Outstanding people have one thing in common: an absolute sense of mission."

Zig Zigglar

7

Mission

The Powerful 3: My Mission

As you are pondering your newly found beliefs, affirmations, supporting stories, you are probably wondering what your life's mission is or should be.

To help you narrow it down and help you create focus and attention you need to create your powerful three driving forces, your "why am I doing this" objectives. You may know the answers right now and they may come easy for you, you can simply write them down.

You may not be quite clear on what these are and that's okay. You can sit down and meditate or focus on them.

If you are like me, meditation sitting down may not help as much. So, go on a walk, alone, in silence (don't be afraid to be alone and in your thoughts, give yourself this breather from the daily hustle and bustle and see what happens) and as you walk focus on the question at hand. Bring the book with you and something to write with, you never know when the stroke of genius will come upon you!

Sidebar – the idea of carrying something to write with and something to write on may be the best gift I have given you here. I have been known to carry this with me all the time and everywhere. The amount of business ideas, book ideas, deals, and so many other things I have solved this way is unsurmountable. It doesn't weigh a ton and it doesn't cost an arm or a leg or a first born. Use it, it could change your life!

What are three things that you need to accomplish by the end of your life, so that when you look back drawing your last breath, you can say that you have lived a fulfilled and happy life? (If the idea of the end of the life may be too big, it's okay to go for a shorter term, say a year or your next big birthday)

1.

2.

3.

What specific action you must take every day or every week that will help you realize above stated objectives?

On Success

The crucial aspect of becoming successful is to define your own success. Many people don't know what their definition of success is, which is why they never feel successful.

You must have your own definition of success, just like you have your own objectives in life. I challenge you to develop your own definition of success.

To help you out, here is my personal definition of success:

To feel and do be better every day and in every way. To do good for the humanity and feel gratitude on daily basis. To continuously grow and improve and to strive to do something every day that makes me smile and laugh. To find beauty in everything.

Now it's your turn.

What's your definition of success? You will know you are

successful when...

When was a time when you felt incredibly successful?

What did you specifically do?

How did you feel when you got there?

Can you breathe the way you did then? Stand the way you

did then. How does it feel reliving it?

Can you repeat it?

It's all cultural

The way we perceive the world around us is created through filters instilled in us through our identities and our cultural backgrounds and upbringings. Everyone experiences the world a bit differently and how we react to certain stimuli can be as much of a cultural response as it is a personally experience based response.

To grasp the concept better, think of how you have witnessed individuals from different communities great each other.

In New York you might greet someone by nodding your

head up slightly and saying "How you doin'?" In Japan, people will bow to each other. Spaniards kiss twice, Serbs kiss three times (it's a luck thing). Americans hug. Some friends scream when they encounter each other after long periods and others cry. And so on.

Most of what we do and how we do it is a learned behavior.

If a behavior is learned and I don't particularly like a certain behavior, then I can change it by learning

If my cultural background is important to me, it is safe to assume that SOME other individuals may feel the same. So, approaching people with the understanding that they might be quite proud of all who they are and their cultural heritage may be very important when meeting people for the first time.

Assuming that everyone is the same just because of their cultural background is often incorrect.

I am only human and as such I will make mistakes. I accept that and I give myself a break. Make sure you do the same for yourself, but also ensure you leave room for others too.

I can help prevent mistakes by not making assumptions, but rather asking questions and doing it with a stance of genuine wanting to know and learn.

How I identify and view myself is important to me and it can very likely be very important to many people I meet.

I must respect other people's identities at face value, even if I don't see it.

When I lived in Southern California, I was fortunate to have Juan as my supervisor. Juan was kind, gentle, funny, and above all accepting of every living creature on this planet. Juan didn't care about what your outer appearance said about you or what your legal document said your name was. Juan cared about who you told him you are and what name you preferred to use. So even if your legal document said your name is George and you appeared to be a male of African descent, but you introduced yourself to Juan as Emilia and you saw yourself as an Afro-Cuban Queen, Juan would treat you as a queen and call you Emilia. He completely embodies the statement of accepting others as they wish to be seen and accepted and I believe we all can be a bit more like Juan, less judging, more loving.

I cannot expect that everyone will understand me, so I must be clear and follow up with questions to ensure alignment.

I cannot expect that everyone communicates or operate in the same way I do and I cannot assume everyone speaks the same language or the same proficiency as me.

The communication and language component is crucial to success. My mentor Joel often tells of a story of a language barrier miscommunication he encountered. His programs are so powerful and his lessons so moving that most people when they invest to study with him do not want their money back ever.

In his demonstration one time he picked a woman he didn't really know and offered her money. To his surprise she took the money, politely thanked him and put it in her purse.

He was very confused but accepted the outcome. He proceeded to ask her a question as to what she was not learning that she would so eagerly take the money back. Her reply: "Sorry, no English."

He still offers money to his students, but he ensures they speak English first now.

The old saying goes: "treat others as you'd like to be treated." While that sounds good, that assumes that everyone wants what I want, which is incorrect. The saying can be improved with our understanding of the cultural and just basic human difference: Treat others as they wish to be treated.

Teach others to treat me as I wish to be treated.

This thought is so good y'all (I say y'all when I really get excited about something, in case you wondered).

We often allow others to treat us however, we give in when we don't really want to. We say it's okay when we are hurt. We feed into the insecurities and train others how treating us should be. Yes, train others!

When you say no to a child and they throw a tantrum and then you give in, you just taught that child that no means scream and you'll get what you want. And every time you repeat the pattern it gets stronger. Then you wonder why do behave the way they do with you.

Same goes for the adults. If you are always on time and other party is always late and you don't say anything and you wait and wait, you are indeed teaching them that you can be at their backing call. Now, this may be absolutely true for you, in which case that's perfectly fine. However, if that's not how you wish things to be, you need to speak up and stand up for yourself.

True story of how I teach others to treat me: I value time. I believe that it's the ONLY commodity we have in unlimited and uncertain quantity and to me time is sacred. If we agree on meeting at a particular time by golly we are meeting at that time. Now, I understand a minute here or there, but overall stick to it. If you're running late or I'm running late (life happens) you call, text, tweet, or send smoke signals if necessary, to get the message out there to the other party.

I had an online meeting with someone with whom I was considering doing business. It would have been great for me, great for them. First meeting went well and we scheduled a second one. I was there, they weren't. I sent a message thinking internet connection went bad, battery died... life happened, right. I waited about 5 minutes then I was gone.

About two hours later or so I get a text message saying sorry I had an important meeting.

What do you think I did? What would you have done?

For me the deal died when they didn't show up and something else become more important and I was an afterthought.

If I moved forward like that, our entire relationship I would have to play a second fiddle and I simply don't do that. I am either number one or I'm not the one and I am perfectly comfortable with either.

More people in the world are different from me than they are the same. It is my task to learn how I can serve both: those who are like me and those who are different.

What are the ways that your identity and cultural upbringings can help you achieve your objectives?

In what ways can you erve those that are different from

you and how can you help them?

What can you do and with whom can you partner with, to attract those who are vastly different from you?

Have you ever made an error when dealing with someone

different from you?

What did you learn from it specifically?

"Success usually comes to those who are too busy to be looking for it."

Henry David Thoreau

Epilogue

A great mentor has taught me a valuable lesson: when someone asks what time is it, it's not about the actual hours, it is about the present time, as once it's gone, it's gone forever.

The Time is NOW!

Time is NOW to step up to the bigger game, to achieve what you know you were born to do, to reach out as many people as you can and spread your message! Time is the most precious asset we will ever have and it's time to stop wasting it and using it to our advantage.

We all have a message and a service for the world. Some

of us serve through offering financing to businesses and individuals, some of us are builders, others are teachers, and there are those who heal us too.

We all have a purpose and mine is to empower people to take action, to do better today than they did yesterday, and to change the financial picture one person, one family, one business at a time.

My purpose is to empower the individuals like you, with families like yours, to become financially independent and able to retire early at any age.

It is your time to get more out of life. It is your time to succeed and achieve. It is your time to live life by your own design and make money work harder for you than you work for it.

Remember all you have to do is make a decision and then go for it!

Until next time, stay Forever Money Blessed!

What Now?

Congratulations! You have been exposed to some of the most powerful and effective techniques, concepts and ideas to become successful.

But no matter how good these ideas and thoughts may be, just being exposed to them is not enough.

You must take action.

I hope that you were filling in the blanks and participating with the book, answering the questions.

Now the real work begins. To get the most value out of this book, you might want to consider developing a step-by-step action plan. An effective and results producing plan should consist of 5 areas:

1. EVALUATION

Ideas are nothing more than ideas until they are put into action. Once acted on, they have the potential to turn around a struggling life or business, or help an already successful individuals become even more dynamic and successful.

Take the time to evaluate what areas and what ideas you are most lacking and could use the most attention.

You have the potential of making the most improvement in your own life, if you will take the time to identify and work on the area of greatest need, first.

Remember the power of one and instead of focusing on so many other things, focus on one thing at a time.

2. RESEARCH

Once you've identified your greatest needs and placed them in priority order, you can begin to search out available solutions.

Be on an opportunity lookout. The material in this book is just the beginning and I hope that you will think many hours on ways that you can impact your own life and life of others for better.

Don't turn any ideas away just because you think they might not pertain to what you want to accomplish. Be open to what comes your way. Capture them, seize the moment and then apply step number three.

3. PERSONALIZATION

As you encounter new ideas, keep an open mind. Study them. Analyze them. And think them through.

When an idea or an opportunity comes your way, ask yourself if it will bring you closer to your overall objective.

If something is presented to you, think whether it's something that you are really excited about or if it's something you just think you "ought to do".

Follow in the footsteps of the wise: If it's not a "heck yeah" it's a no.

Don't be afraid to pass on something that doesn't fulfill you and doesn't lead you where you wish to go.

The material in the book is designed to illustrate concepts and ideas. It is meant to get your juices flowing and empower you to start thinking differently.

4. IMPLEMENTATION

Just as a gym membership won't do its owner any good unless they actually go there and participates in the exercise program, so too, with the information in this book.

It's of no practical use unless it is implemented. It's easy to come up with good ideas and develop plans, but where most people get bogged down is when it comes to putting them into action and implementing.

It's not always easy, but if you're going to truly be successful, you must do whatever it takes to act on your plans.

Read the book at least once a year, especially your own answers. It will continue to inspire you and drive you.

5. REVIEW

After you've worked with your new ideas for a period of time, pause and evaluate how things are working.

You may need to make some adjustments so you can continue to see improvement and growth.

Sometimes, an idea you thought was great doesn't work out at all. That's okay, don't continue using it. Just scrap it and move on to something else.

On the other hand, if you find an idea that works well, see if you can refine it and maximize it to make it even more effective.

I understand that journey to your outcome may feel like a lot. There is a lot to do and many strategies to be implemented.

The said truth is that majority of the individuals who get the book won't get this far. The few that will won't take any action. They will remain in the Never Land in the Nation of Procrasta.

On one hand that's very unfortunate, because if they would only get out of their own way they could be even more successful.

On the other hand, their failure to take action is good for you.

1% doesn't become the 1% because everyone else does it. No! They are the one-percenters because the remaining 99% does nothing. By taking an action, you actually have a great chance to become the top elite of doers, achievers, and most successful people in the world.

You have the tools. You have the tip. You have the techniques and mission. All is left is to…

GO FOR YOUR DREAMS!

What is your ONE THING you'd like to get started on right now?

What objective do you want to achieve?

How will you feel when you reach your objective?

In your minds eye, see yourself achieving your objective.
Breathe as if you have achieved it.

Stand the way you stand when you achieve an objective
you have set for yourself.

Is there something to taste or smell where you are in your
minds eye of success? Taste it. Smell it. What does it taste
like? What does it smell like?

Are there any sounds? What are they? In your minds eye
make the sounds even louder.

How does it feel to have the objective accomplished?

What stories are you telling others about your journey to the objective?

What is stopping you from getting your objective acomplished? Feeling the success? Tasting it? Smelling it? Hearing it?

What specifically are you committing to do to make it happen?

Additional Products from Nev

BOOKS
"From Financially Stressed To Money Blessed: Become Financially Independent and Retire Early At Any Age"
Available on Amazon.com

"Creating Customers For Life"
Available in gift form ONLY, typically at my live events.

EDUCATION
"Instant Wealth"
Online and live education system for those looking to invest for passive income.
Visit: 1DealAway.com

"Money Matters"
Online and live education system for those who wish to master their money.
Visit: 1DealAway.com

"Real Street MBA"
Online and live education system designed to transform your financial life and set you financially independent.
Visit: 1DealAway.com

"Investing4Million$ MasterClass"
Real Estate Investing Mastery Course.
By Application ONLY.
E-mail: UR1DealAway@gmail.com, codeword: **"Million$"**

As a THANK YOU for reading this book, I'd like to personally invite you to my **$1,997** per ticket, Live Event: "Instant Wealth"

To receive **2 FREE** tickets, email codeword: "FIRE" In subject line and send

To
UR1DealAway@gmail.com

Nev holds a Bachelor's and Master's in Business Administration, has been building businesses, investing, teaching and empowering individuals for over 20 years.